I CAN'T FIND ME

Ni Allaf Ddod O Hyd I Hyn

יתוא אוצמל לוכי אל

თავს ვერ ვპოულობ

DOMINIC STEVENSON

Winter Goose
PUBLISHING
where words take flight

Winter Goose Publishing
45 Lafayette Road #114
North Hampton, NH 03862

www.wintergoosepublishing.com
Contact Information: info@wintergoosepublishing.com

I Can't Find Me

COPYRIGHT © 2016 by Dominic Stevenson

First Edition, April 2016

Cover Design by Winter Goose Publishing
Typesetting by Odyssey Books

ISBN: 978-1-941058-44-2

Published in the United States of America

Happiness is happening
The dragons have been bled
Gentleness is everywhere
Fear's just in your Head

—David Bowie (1947-2016)

To those who believe in adventure

To the steady hand that stopped me chasing a dream,
disordered and chaotic,
and guided me here

To today, and tomorrow

Contents

ONE

At My Birth

I will kiss you with my mother tongue,
Byddaf yn cusanu chi gyda fy mamiaith,
ימא תפשב דתוא קשנא ינא,
მშობლიური ენით გაკოცებ,
drench your soil with sweat of brow by day,
drensho'ch pridd gyda chwys ael y dydd,
השקה יתדובע תעיזב דתמדא תא ביטרא,
შენს ნიადაგს მზის ოფლით მოვრწყავ,
and sleep beneath your stars.
a cysgu o dan eich sêr.
דייבכוכ תחת ןשאו.
შენს ვარსკვლავიან ცას გადავიფარებ.

I'll never be alone
Wna i byth fod ar fy hun
דבל היהא אל םלועל
არასოდეს ვიქნები მარტო,
while your clouds pour rain on
tra bod eich cymylau'n arllwys glaw
לע םשג ופטשי דיינעעש העשב
სანამ შენი ღრუბლები ჩემს ოცნებებს ნამავენ.
my dreams that tomorrow will be a better day.
ar fy mreuddwydion y bydd yfory yn ddiwrnod gwell.
רתוי בוט םוי היהי רחמש ייתומולח.
ოცნებებს, რომ ხვალ უკეთესი დღე იქნება.

Written by Dominic Stevenson and translated into Georgian by visual artist Mariam Natroshvili, into Hebrew by playwright Lilac Yosiphon, and into Welsh by poet Joao Morais.

One, or as Close to, It Began

You cannot fight for peace,
but you can write for it.
Fall to knee
and run your fingers,
worn by industry
and smoothed by the caresses of your lover's cheek,
through the green torn stems of grass—sweet the morning
milk of dew.

When praising the immortal,
when presiding with the immortal,
when praising the unquestioned,
when presiding with the unquestioned,
you only see through your damaged eyes
scarred by others' soulless interpretations of our sacred kisses
from above.

It's no guidebook to your city.
It's civilian and divisive and teaches you wrong.
Only lessons learnt by examining the consequences, and
effect on others, of your action can fill your blank pages.
Positive, go again.
Negative, apologise, learn, and move on.
Let all read your book,
but make none follow it to the letter.
Your times, your errors and your kindnesses, make for your
days

full to burst with what you deserve
and all must learn to write their own.

No divinity lives and loves in each life story, but kisses from
the ones we crave to kiss fill our water tower brains, leaning
treacherously above our mass and making us omniscient.

Two Journeys

The faux fur lined coat,
grey scarf, red scarf, black and red scarf, tiger striped Con-
verse and turquoise bowl hat, pink scarf, black rimmed
glasses, another faux fur coat collar and a thick-eared grin
to bounce off the terror that friendship throws. This is what
makes those sat around me blankly following the curvature
of the deadly dark descending tunnel through which we're all
travelling at thirty-seven MPH.

The manbird stands on the platform edge, silently tail-fan-
ning his feathers for praise and gold statuettes. We stop,
observe, and fly on ourselves—back at break neck speed, we
away and wobble and see the light together, as one.
Smashing the darkness with our hope to see the one we crave
to kiss again.

Your light blisters my skin.
The subjectivity of your dutiful subject
sees harm in your presence.
Lead from room to room,
shepherded by handbag clutching
bowers who don't even call you by your name.
The chosen one by God,
or so we are told,
or the one in the right place,
the right scarf,
the right time in which you bleed your name,

and lose your virtue,
blood red onto pages of manuscript until paper is your friend
no more.

Does your every footstep pound for the betterment of those
forced to kneel,
or did the call of history beat your conscience to it?

Three Letters Introduce the River

You aren't the Thames,
wading through the smoke chimneys of someone's youth,
and someone's crisis, and someone's last days.
You aren't a vital artery in this land while you read that book
ignoring what is forcefully etched in your taut muscular flesh
by life and those you live with.

Pull the curtains on the whirring of the fan
and the choke of the car that the chef in whites,
too skinny to trust with his rubbish sack of microwave food
wrappers,
sits in to smoke his cigarettes while on his break.
Royal blue, heavy, but not blackout,
they keep most of the pollution at bay but through the cracks
seeps a reminder that you're not in control of the world
beyond the window.

Drag your trailer of junk
down the stairs and out your door.
Lay it out for the bin men,
the refuge seekers on a scrap above the minimum, who won't
take a load if the lid is too high.
It's too much to drag from place to place, with too many
faces staring up from the letters and photographs, frayed but
still poignant through the fog of the mind.

When you dare out
to the town of home and family
and go walking down the beachhead,
do you see Noah and feel his
Atlantic kiss wash your sin as the
battle of water smacking sand and sea wall
continues to ravish the promenade? Do you see a
dove seeking refuge and
entire families huddling in the arms of their

> matriarch

fighting onward above the churn, with the
geese soon gone for winter? Do you see the
harrowing glare of the hungry aimed at the
Indian takeaway wrappers, disgust, a
job for the
kestrel? Picking through their mire.
Love you
must, to keep the blood pumping.
Noah calls each, two by two.
Oceans to cross,
ponds calm as the pigeon chases.
Quantity of boatload knows no bounds.
Robin,
sparrow,
therapods, in their early form, didn't make the cut.
Understanding
vultures waited to last.
Wet and patient,
x-raying the crowd but seeing none lame enough

> on which to feast.

Yellow sun begins to shine and the battle of man

is lost.

Zulu drums, heard last in noble times, beat the

animals farewell. Again.

Four Steps

Whisper. The last words of the mermaid.
Hoisted seafaring legs
kick high in protest
at enforced land.
Cwtch is the waves
passed down, blue, green,
as flesh as her father,
mother, pained watching
her sequel. Ripped from
the womb, stolen.
A plethora of life bobbed behind
striking out at tomorrow
she reached out to
caress today. Or
what was left of it.
No mermaid, but a
woman in love with
Poseidon poisoned to
the preacher's kiss
and crawling land
up skirt misery. Right.
A cry. A cry. A cry
of a child sent to
say goodbye. At
dawn of the next
the panting stopped
as with her eyes

she forewarned
rage and suffering
for grace and
godliness that her
legs could not stand
on this land.
They buried her in
a field. And she
lay, kicking out.

Five Strikes on Terra Firma and You're Out

Under the clay tomb
frantic you and I, stand.
Suited dominoes,
tweed, classic outfits of our time
except me in trainers, you in your polished to the finite black
loafers.
Your arms dart side and up,
into, and out of, your pockets
while my head jerks keeping time with the four beats before
death that ring out like the
cock crow in my head.
While they spell doom if we don't dance, I fear you're the
same my new friend—only more pronounced.

I'm a nodding bobble head,
and you're an underground disco diva,
but we've been afflicted so long we have forgotten what it
feels like to give two hoots about the stares. We're grateful for
the extra room at rush hour as no one dares stand by, just in
case, you know . . .
we read one of those books, that we were vulnerable, and
that we spell your end with our manic smiles and shakes.

We don't long for anything,
time and a compass to the back
between where my angel wings will sprout,
we don't miss love, nor long for something at the end.
Us, the movers and shakers, we're not doing too badly.

Six Lines Drawn on My Face

He sits down opposite, but
it's too early for me to make him a new smile,
so I lend him one of mine.
Across the walkway down the middle of the train I hand her
a cheesy one, a warm one,
a few sizes too big and second hand.
But a smile for him to wear, if he ever so wishes.

Seven, When the Sun Doesn't Shine

Some faces in the crowd
always draw a frown
on the wind that whispers
what today holds
and blows the best laid
into the fresh pages of tomorrow.

Eyes flicker behind painted features,
examining the morning respirations of those near,
looking to openly condemn a slither of joy oozing into the
still dark surroundings of the communal of mass movement.

A mouth that you can't imagine
climbing the peaks of happiness
at its furthest points.
Stuck. Destined to be ruled straight,
but by expectation, sadness, or fear?

Some live for the furrowed forehead,
but what happens on the good days?
What happens when they make love?
Are they still monsters of the ice
whistling their miserable tune into the north wind?

You were the midnight *tick tock*
that fell upon the ears of this land
and drowned it in your sin.

You kissed the people crushed 'neath actions of utmost cruelty, one by one, lipstick stains corrosive on their pure flesh.

You stalked the corridors
closing down chatter, debate,
because it's subversive.
It kicks out at your rule.

Say goodbye,
we shall not die.
Forever building
bodies making fertile ground
for growth.

Eight Ways to Skin the Snakes

When I am born again,
at the writing desk of someone who questions what it must
have been like to be in that time, place, know I will scream
from the page at that child.
I will tell them to leave the page and go and play and learn
how to be heartbroken amongst friends and how to build a
tower of regrets only to rename them successes in the guise of
sadness.
Nothing was learnt indoors,
that is a place for those who fear the terror of cuddles and
supper by candlelight.
If you go out armed,
with ink smudges on your fingers and paper in your back
pocket, then you will take the day and leave it wrapped in
posterity to help ease the next into their adulthood.

Nine Stops to Home

You followed me,
and sat beside my aching self,
with the knees of your leather trousers.
Well, not leather, but some kind of material that I can't
name,
knees worn and bare of thread like the trousers of a sinner.
They're torn and they don't match the rest of your immacu-
late dress.
One adorable mole to the right of your plump lips, and one
on the right of the bridge of your nose.
I watched your reflection.
You know I'm sat on the Northern Line,
between Kings Cross and Camden Town,
writing about you
but you don't care.
You're so sublime you've been a million artists' muse,
yet you've never seen a single portrait of yourself
and so you hold my gaze hoping that I'll flip my phone, my
pad, my mind so I can share my thoughts with you.

Gaudi knelt at the altar of his church,
that would remain unfinished from that day to this.
One night he fell beneath the wheels of the Number 30
tram,
and died as a pauper in hospital
only to be recognised by kin and buried beneath his black-
ened spires.

Come tomorrow, for we will do beautiful things.
We will build this monument to tower
and shower us in the luxury of eternity
no longer lost on the seven straight roads where redemption
is the only end—but now free to die and be forgotten once
the world around your corpse carries on spinning when your
flesh rots and burns and becomes the ashes that feed the trees
or the fishes.

Ten Mysteries Never Solved

It must be fun to pretend to be a dog.
I am doing it right now.
Hands soaped,
knees scrapped,
waiting for a train
panting and anxious to get into the right spot to my entrance
meets my exit and
limits my walking at destination.
If I could smash through the reinforced double sheet of glass
to stick my head into the noxious wind whipping through
the tunnel so that my tongue can hang loose and saliva mark
my trail south,
then I would.

Silence.

At My Death

It's been days since I've returned to these pages,
but like a third degree
they're still here.
The grace,
and in the trace of all I do,
as I pen my heart
with indelible ink onto the whiteness of this ocean of pulp.

As I turned my back on it all,
the beauties and the terrors of my time in this place,
I put my hand in my pocket
and to my surprise,
I found a fossil.
Bringing it close to my eyes
I whispered to it:
From where have you come?
It didn't answer,
but in its charred blackness
I saw my last smile—
the one I gave away,
so onward I marched.

I've never looked back.

I never did find me.

TWO

Flesh

Where? But crumbled flesh
bleeding the light beneath the balustrades,
crawling from blue mist
of royal hue
to a broken dawn
to lay upon heels clicked
making flight of fancy
over burnt towns
and flaming children.

When? Before your kin
gave a thought to baby
blue and pink
with choking breath.
Stained like a passer by
to a vicious wound sustained
in an act of love.

Why? Because you must.

Sweet Dreams Baby

See you in the morning
he bellowed into the landing,
making sure that all in the house
knew his bed beckoned.

No one shouted back,
but in time
pale cheeks,
streaked with black,
would lean over the edge of the crib
and tuck him in.

Self-contained,
restrained from midnight revelry
by bed linen pulled tight,
and teddy bears standing guard.
Saluted by the drowsy general,
none shall pass
until he stands them down at
the sunrise hour.

As he takes one final examining gaze around the room,
with hand crafted, and painted, aeroplanes hanging from the
ceiling
fighting for neutral airspace with plastic covered in shiny
silver paper.
His big boy pants keep him

secure in the manhood of dryness,
sinking the possibility
of childlike mannerisms being exposed.

His flaccid cheeks
turn red overnight
as the heating stays on an hour late,
and comes on an hour early,
to take the bite out of the winter chill.

When he wakes,
he reaches out
to be swooped up.
She holds him,
squeezing her son close to her chest,
and shakes.

Black streaks
down pale cheeks.

You Can't Tell a Child
That Mountains Can't Wait

Mountain wait

for the sun to crawl to its peak.
Upon reaching the summit,
it watches by the dead zone,
as it stirs into life
the villages at its feet.
Children dance,
warmed by rays
that fill their tiny
uncorrupted spirits to the brim,
as they bound to see
morning light glisten on the peak's snow.

As the sun climbs back
up the mountain,
its slithering fingers
gliding back over
the rooftop glacier,
the children who now sleep,
are remembered in the darkness
by footprints in the mud.

What Is the Value of Life
When Nectar Is the Other Choice?

We all wish we were addicted
to something sweet,
straight to the vein.
We wish,
we wish that there were no consequences—
then we could dance
to Lou Reed,
the Velvet Underground,
in the same entrapment of spirit
that they wrote in.
We'd shake our arms and legs to Pulp,
like Jarvis intended
when he spoke of our mis-shaped youth.
We homage with a thrust of the hips,
a pull to the dance floor
on the arm of a girl with curls
and a smile we'd always write about in
the notebooks battered,
carried around in our bags
to the nine-to-five.
Sodding the consequences
with plastic pint glasses
and screaming in the faces of strangers
because each night
was ours,
and we'll never get over that.

Addicted to life,
instead of the pulse pumping
needle sticking that inspired the heroes of ours
who showed us the way it could be,
if we didn't have to wake up
to a call from those we loved enough
not to betray them with recklessness.
We all wish we were addicted to something
that would take us away,
offering the serenity of creating,
with the long life.
No one wants to burn out like Kurt or Amy,
we want to live and thrive and
be alive to hear and tell the stories
of the people who went the extra mile
and took the herbs and essence of earth
finding a different way to consume,
instead of valuing that
being left in the head was as easy
as opening the eyes
because I guarantee that Mother Nature leaves us
with more sincere psychedelics than Lennon ever knew.
Take the prick in the arm,
the pint with a chaser,
the powder or the pill,
but I promise,
when I looked in her eyes
I lived it all.
But pretend addicts don't get
headlines,
like Hoffman.

That's what we envy.
Surrounded by downfall,
his dignity shattered
when brown entered his vein,
red left,
out of control,
at the bottom of a spiral,
seeking help and climbing the walls.
Trying abstinence
Wasn't enough this time.
Beyond his demons now,
small mercy for great genius.
It's the daydream
with which we're more concerned,
who'd write our obituary,
and who'd sell their stories of our sin,
instead of reflecting on the luxury of peace of mind.
And we despair
for empty space
where own column inches
could have been.

Poison (A Pauper's Realisation)

Scrape the skin,
spike my vein,
with your goodwill.
Slide it deep
Pierce me,
fill me
with your
poison brown
until I collapse
with the realisation
that my best interests
were not yours.

Eyes fall level with
the mattress,
sordid stains
overflowing
its smooth cream wrapper,
and I watch you
walk on.

Junk

I stood back and watched
you leave dark green poisoned footsteps
in the pale hued frost crusted grass,
marking where you were about to go.
Inch by inch,
a life foretold to the end.
I hope that when death delivers you on the road to Hades,
that he will look back,
just once,
mourning his own work.

Simon Says

Shirley says:
Stop talking about Simon.

Shirley says:
Stay silent.
Why must I
walk through my door
into the street
baring my breasts,
or thighs,
to satisfy Simon's eyes
as he hollers my way?

Shirley says:
Scrap your preconceptions.
I got a better degree than Simon,
my work experience
isn't just parlance
to please,
let me off my knees.
I beg.
Why does Simon own more zeros than me?

Shirley says:
Stop telling me I need a man.
Simon kissed me quick.
But he never asked,

just took,
expecting a shag,
and when I smacked him with my bag,
his mates laughed.

Shirley says:
No.

Simon says:
So?

Shirley says:
I can't,
I'm busy.

Shirley says:
nothing any more.
But no one asks why.

Simon says:
what goes.

Let Me Break My Wheels

This poem is a fictional adaptation of first-hand accounts of abuse

It's the cycle of care
that I do not dare,
stop.

No.

Wait man.

It wasn't my fault.

Born into it
by my mum—
she did drink,
and my dad—
he did hit.
He hit,
and he hit,
and he tore our house down.

With tears decorating
the walls,
and the dresses
of me and his missus,
we screamed and we danced

making howls to the night
with the glint of the moonlight
from an upended bottle
illuminating the only land he'd let us know.

Standing in my pyjamas
at the bottom of the stairs,
with my only care,
the cry of my mum.

Her feet slashed
and dripping with blood
as I pulled up the hood
of my dressing gown.
But I was only a kid,
I had to stay hid,
but I couldn't.

My feet ripping too,
on the broken Chardonnay bottle,
and he began to throttle
mum.
Then he hit
and he hit
and he pulled her hair out.

They had loved since school
but he never wanted me,
he just wanted to rule
and so she had to protect her womb cradle
for me to grow,

but nobody knew then
that he'd hit
and he'd hit
and he'd fracture my skull.

Now I can't see my mum,
he struck her too dumb.
She lives by the wine
and cider and beer and spirits
that charge the fire in her belly,
where I had once grown.

I'm told I'm a waste,
and won't achieve much,
but you've got me all wrong.
If my bones can heal
and my heart can mend,
then just round the bend
lives my hope.

I'll study hard to get away,
and stay away,
from the cycle of care,
that stranded me here.

My Feet Only Define Me in Your Eyes

Native born. Nature bred.
Dancing in the streets over broken window panes
and splinters from the frames
they spy me.
Spray paint decorates our house
with crude words,
spelt badly.
Youthful enthusing of life
tip
tapping
from my toes
infecting the cobbles and slabs of concrete,
somehow it was their business.
They thought I was ill,
in need of a cure.
My neighbour,
the physician,
bled me.
His fist,
a leech on my eyelid,
blood
drip
drip
drop
decorating my fallen smile,
with the twinkle
of my winkle pickers

tarnished.
I tip
tapped
no more.

Delight on the Shoulder of a Giant

I let go of your sparrow ankle,
slung over my shoulder,
and tiny hands clawed into my cheeks.

You screeched,
but I ignored you,
continuing to reach
for what I saw as more pressing:
a little girl balancing on a wall,
not the one securely on my shoulders.

You didn't let me go
you whispered in my ear.

Never
I replied.

You didn't hurt me
in gentle, relieved tones.

Never
I replied.

Her body smiled,
thighs clenching my ears in
childish delight,
trusting me,

and she gripped my cheeks again
before asking if she was the kind of girl
I'd want as a daughter.

My Value

I didn't know what was important
until an eight-year-old
who'd already been beaten
black and blue
by life
asked if she was the kind of daughter
I'd want as my own.

Tears streamed
as I spoke of her needing a grown-up,
not a child in a man suit—
with a beard and unearned flecks of grey atop—
to help her move forward
into her own adolescence
and independence.

What good are you really,
if at every challenge
to your quo,
you have to explain yourself away,
and tell tales of your unsuitability,
and vulnerability?

Take the challenge,
run through hell to
slash your cloth
and force a smile from a grimace
and make a difference.

Living with the Past

The lady on the train
opened all her birthday cards,
and smiled,
alone.
One from her child.
Rip,
pull,
open,
read,
smile,
reinsert,
put back in bag.
One from her brother.
Rip,
pull,
open,
close,
open,
read,
smile,
reinsert,
put back in bag.
One from a school friend.
Rip,
pull,
open,
read,

smile,
reread,
reinsert,
put back in bag.
One from her mother.
Rip,
pull,
open,
read,
lift and smell,
smile,
reinsert,
put back in bag.
With all of her wishes
wrapped up in torn paper,
and in a canvas bag,
she was alone now
but for me as company.
I wept for her
and her envelopes.
Empty,
this card opening lady on a train.

THREE

Nature Creeping Up the Walls
Could Not Protect Him

He grew ivy up,
and down,
the length of each wall
letting it grow over
every ceiling too,
so that they couldn't get in.
He even let it grow around his feet,
so that they couldn't rise from below
and confront him.
Ghosts can't get past nature.
They can't penetrate,
when all around is the Mother's purity.
Like a glove that God slid over pain,
tenderly,
to protect
her fragile creation,
ivy grew
enveloping all it encountered.
Sitting in the middle of the room,
walls crawling,
shifting with life,
he tapped his heel
and waited.

But waiting for nothing
can be more damaging

than not waiting
and being torn.

Shredded by the ghosts
who carry your fears,
in a postman's satchel,
delivering them
into your hand.
The growth of his solitude,
matched that of the ivy, which would
eventually ensnare him.
Suffocating the last gasps of air
from his lungs
and casting him to the heavens,
untouched there by the arrival of
truths carried by poltergeist.
But unfulfilled,
and with so many answers yet to find,
his god.

She chose to keep him
in his ivy chamber,
as a white cloaked reminder
to push people to live.
The man wrapped in ivy
lives on, again, still.

Can You Reach the Monastery?

where Jesus wept

                                    he tasted nectar at the last

                     and

walking through gardens of plums

                              knew his days were marked.

kissing the sky the

                                      pure, content

                     poor

rich in gold is man now

                     he arrived hoisting each arm high

faint but for his feet

               comfortable that he was the kin of all men

                   now

callous, irregular

                                  flushed crimson

no path gone astray this

                  worthy of the beginning of time

                  day

a king, divine build on a

                       a leader born into folk love.

Disturbed

Porlock on the days of sin,
Porlock when my fingers begin
to talk of the days,
when Jesus wept with his Uncle
at Glastonbury Tor.
I'd dreamt of a war,
like never before,
to knock the wheat from the chaff.
Then I'd woken with a shock
the horror before my eyes,
still shut
from day
our daily bread
not yet a thought in my head.
But if a single soul fell in my name,
I would put the pennies on their eyes
and carry them across to eternity myself.
The dead would lay on my heart,
a burden on the conscience that would
haunt
until my final breath.

Porlock women.

Porlock men.

Porlock travellers knocking at my door.

Save me from the grasp of greatness,
keep my soul from a timeless
weightlessness,
on the shelves
I'd forever dwell
near the bottom right,
with the rest of the esses.

Wonderland, Wonderland

She grabbed my hand,
nails digging into me for leverage,
and she swung herself
into the air,
knowing I wouldn't let her go.

She was dancing in her Wonderland,
she was prancing in her Wonderland.

Eyes glazed,
she gazed,
far past today,
distancing herself from me,
holding her,
palm on palm.

With her far off stare
she never let me forget,
just how fragile we were—
as I stopped her flying to infinity,
limiting her,
saving her.

While she twirled in the air around me,
with legs gracefully kicking,
hair flailing in the current of atmosphere,
and her breath held with excitement,
she was beautiful,

but cold.

You can't keep a girl from her wonderland.

False Roots

When I go into battle,
my skin, scales,
roar, raw
against the brown valleys,
and grey cities,
of home.

A Dragon I am.

Three Eternities

Winchester's geese sleep, with the unknown children they keep warm, in the dark mud beneath slabs of granite. Tread quietly.

When the sunshine broke through grey clouds, steam made wings of his shoulders, he knew he'd not turn around to say goodbye.

My heart skipped a beat when yours skipped two. You grabbed your right arm and fell. Staring up at me, we began to weep. Goodbye.

Class War

Stars on your own,
walking alone,
crying out to the streets
to hear you.

You've taken a shot,
at being the one,
to speak for your neighbours
and kin.

But you're not alike,
they only care for the quo,
and they'll nod and curtsey at will.
Strike no fear in the heart,
of those who have none,
it matches the notes in their purse.

There is no war,
like the class war,
but only the generals unite.

The privates they stand,
and grin oh so grand,
whenever the piano strikes up.
They'll sing
and they'll march,
and parade up and down
never to be met with a frown.

As families applaud
their free flights abroad,
natives of lands
that are still in the hands
quiver at the sight of their wave.

Happy and glorious,
she stands over more of us,
than we even realise.
At least fifteen peoples of earth,
live in a dearth,
where only her tune rings out.

So God save the queen,
a whimsical regime,
that should have died out with the last.

It ain't the fault of old Lizzie,
but they should get busy,
and retire to Balmoral or Windsor or Kensington or even
flammin' Kennington,
just as long as they don't cost me a thing.

I'm fed up of wasting,
even a quid a year
to keep the old dear
in rags.

She's not my concern,
and I'd rather burn,
the paper bearing her face,
than kneel.

My passport it says,
she gives me free pass,
but I'd rather be liked by the world.

Not a plane trip goes by,
where you and I,
don't see the problems they caused.
If it's not famine
It's God,
those silly old sods,
went and messed up
too much to be true.

We all should hold hands,
and slowly demand,
that our freedom is our right,
they should lower their might,
given from lands of the poor.

Drowning in the Liffey

I give you lad
the end of my sin,
seen through bifocal glass bottoms.
Staying and praying are not noble,
They're the defeat of a man's spirit,
drowning in the Liffey
feeling the burn of the cross
scolding hands that clutch at the sadness and madness
but the water will soak and expand
and retract then crack
your masonry façade
and you'll fly, my son,
not look back,
swallow my sin down
and pass it to your kin.
Watch as wilted eyes fade
and mistakes are made again.
Fall to your knees and
beg another way today.
Beg another way.

Owls

Two owls sit,
bookends on a five bar fence,
guardians of the rolling
ploughed earth.

Their prey scurries unknowingly beneath
where their talons grip,
seconds from death
but they can't raise their necks to see
the silent danger casting a shadow over their tomorrow.
An easy meal for a hungry heart
can't stir the thinkers
whose job it is to watch over
the last of the land left green
by the horror show of the farmers, the bankers—the absolute
atrocities of men
who pillaged their kin.

In the distance,
beneath the smoke stack of the city,
groaning wallets eyed this turf
and its owl centurions,
but turned their backs once more
to look at the raging pavements
below.
Electronic books don't burn
but banknotes do,

and as the streets danced with the shadows
of the flames of the revolution,
the faces of power turned to ash.

Trampled on
and kicked into dust
to be swallowed by those running
for their lives.

And it turned out that there was a little bit of owl in all of us.

Battle of Children

Battlefield, battlefield,
my playground in the days of childish
endeavour beneath the
tree and the bow, and the
hunched up mono brow
overhanging
my jumping with joy.
As the time went by
I let life chisel at me.
The blade, with each
hammer blow,
fracturing.

I became the pointed definition
of a bullet,
and everyone around me started to wear
a round white
and red
target on their faces—
both of them.
With a rage,
in a haze,
I've taken my hate out on you.

Standing there
stopping to stare,
but never seeing my weep.

As it came to pass
you never did mass
the courage to stand
up and free me.
The sole survivor of the ten thousand mundane days
that wetted and wiped my slate clean
for the factory floor bosses to fill with booze and destruction.
I'm fighting back.
They couldn't write
my pages for me.

The time of crafting
was mine
and as I look back
I see bodies scattered
with half scrawled messages
of subjugation
tattooing their
picked at silk smoothed skin.

Wallflower

Sometimes the wallflower is just watching and enjoying
people being happy.
As you throw shapes
I don't dream of calm,
but rather of debauch with reason
not dictated by the popular beats,
because my inner rhythm—
while not letting me tap my feet or wave my arms in time—
thuds and bumps
and builds my heart strong
but volatile,
so don't consider me a lone
while my eyes follow feet, hips and fingertips tracing
tomorrow in the skies.
I am quiet,
but I weep for none.

FOUR

Our Town

My aching stick
holding my war worn
battered and torn
body upright
I heard you
out my open window.
Shuffling toward the wooden sill,
I saw you
framed in the street
with the *tip-tap*
of your feet
dancing in
and out
the shadows.

I wept.
As you reached the middle distance,
footsteps getting quieter,
I was forced to strain for the music,
and I realised you couldn't see the danger.
Though the moon shone brighter
as midnight clouds parted,
you didn't turn around to see
my frantic arms
windmill in anticipation
of the blows.
And as a furnace of powder grey hell

gurgled from the left
lurching across asphalt,
with filed down teeth twinkling like Sunday service angels,
toward you
I lower my arms defeated and turned.

I couldn't see another go down,
I couldn't watch the rage fill our town.

Marlowe

The ghosts that play the bard
of the Deptford Tavern,
wield their characters once again,
shrouded by darkness
beneath a high rise of influence.
More lovely than in the day of beast
slaughtered at the door to feed
the need of audience aghast,
a thousand candles flicker on
a sheet of water that drowns
the foundation stone of language
in love and protection
from the smoke stacks
and hacks that float above.
Echo of boot on wood beneath hay
bellows through modern ear
calling change through the ages,
forebears glorious in drunk and dance
kicking at the ages,
they've been waiting in the wings too long.
No gloomy look at Sundays fears
strange games they do play there,
storming wigs and dresses of colour
aching to see the sunshine in
through glass or open window alike.
When I walk along the stream now,
I see worship of the other,

who lived longer and wrote for history,
but I know that there is a place,
as the other would have wanted,
for both sets of long gone players
to once again speak the words of truth,
as seen,
once upon a day in London town.

Children

I won't have children in this city.

Managing the trek
to Southwark
from Muswell Hill,
and back again,
is so far as my 16/20 eyes can
see:
the expected inevitably of my semen
and unknown's egg,
deciding that enough dancing around the issue is enough,
then making a future,
is enough to sicken me.

Closed down Sure Start,
so Montessori is a must
then with inner city school toil,
and outer borough work,
their minds weaken.
Pen in worn text book
to down the alley suck,
of a straw from a cider bottle,
as they realise that this city
is boring, lame, rubbish Dad.

They don't deserve to swank
around this town while

I still have the legs to muster crawl from North to East, or
South to West,
buzz fuelled chasing
pop up hopes selling
the next big dream,
once brought in from the docks of Rotherhithe,
now mass produced in a warehouse in Dagenham.

I won't have children in this city.
I'll keep it all to myself.

London Walks

London,
It's been here so long
that we,
those who walk the streets,
don't own it.
We can't carve our own way.
Instead we walk the path of king and pauper
forging forth
because the past is taken.
Pepys documented the meandering of time
and before him
Shakespeare scaled the walls
with his words
and brought the geese to the court
before they were thrown back again
when their penny entry expired.
In recent years
men from the sky threw destruction
and death amongst us,
and miners and nurses and teachers and students and public
workers, freedom fighters and those of all walks
have marched from where Nelson watches,
to where power sits
dipping its toes in the eternal artery.
Now even with the weight of this,
you'll still find a tavern
and down a few

declaring yourself king of the town,
and think you were the first
as you board the 134
North and home.

Our Guide

What would our streets be
without our guide?
Telling us of
the land beneath our feet
and the walls that limit our sideward step.

She wheeled her bike
along the cobbles,
pointing out sites of interest,
slowly revealing
what brought her here.

We fight the revelations,
the truth of our neighbourhood.

Whispering secrets
that bounce off lampposts
and impale us on
paving slabs,
choking us
as we dare to comprehend.
Taking the breadth of her experience,
she slowly,
with an elegance that no onlooker could muster,
removes the cataracts
that blinded,
to help us see.

Another day
we'd have walked on by.

Another day,
we might.

Jack Cinnamon Sleeps in Hampstead Heath

On Jack Cinnamon's bench
a cooling breeze
on the second hottest day of the year
carries the chirping of crickets
past me,
and into the wilds of the heath.
Grandparents encourage toddlers,
who wobble
dangerously close to the lake edge,
to throw bread
to the ducks
so well fed
that they look on impassively.
Jack,
as far gone now
as lived,
would recognise the scene.
A parity in class,
revelling in the grass,
the well-aged lands
free to the community
and visitors alike.
I wonder if Jack was a remarkable man
or if he just liked a view,
and to inspire?

A Puppy on the Northern Line

She was cute,
one of those girls who wore
a pensive,
hard staring
quizzical look
as she read the horoscope in the free newspaper.
The only time her grimace turned to a smile,
one that beamed and set the tube aflame,
was when someone took an interest in her pug.
Her hair,
an inch from the bleach,
fell lazily over her
blusher stained cheek
caressing the undercarriage of her face,
and it made my hair stand on end.
She took that dog on the 9:17 a.m. tube,
from Highgate to Warren Street every day.
I don't know where she was going,
and I could never ask,
because I don't think dogs should be allowed on the tube
given the amount of people with animal fur allergies.

Crumbling Victorian Sewers

Rusting pipes
siphon away the evidence
and guilt
of your bad diet
and drink
down the tunnels,
beneath your feet,
that were built
by the hands
of navvies
a century and a half ago.
They hide away your gluttony,
and fool you that the best is yet to come.

We Devastated the Poor Lands

It's the poor that are left
behind to pick up
the wreck
of the day.

As three hundred cram onto
a steel-frame underground train,
millions more
scuttle above.

Daily grind
doesn't wear us
down
to their level,
beneath the streets
to save a minute,
then earn a pound
for someone else.

Despite the poverty,
who has freedom?
When was the last time they were thanked?
But it's so virtuous
to make profit
irrespective of gain.
So we don't need to.

When we're done with our day
we strut
their streets,
smash bottles,
complete with liquor dregs,
against their window shutters,
then throw up in their doorways.

Next morning,
we stroll past
and comment on their
dirty streets,
uncouth ways,
and watch them
pick up
the wreck of
their day.

Freeman Street

Just come and walk down Freeman street.
See the segregation and
derogation of my birth right.

Shop shutters,
grey like the dawn that broke
over the whole town
when the last trawler landed,
sleep,
make-up drawn on by disenfranchised youth
who know that tomorrow
will mean no better.

The gutter overspill which discolours walls,
as rain water washes pain down the buildings
and floods the pavements with misery induced societal sin,
is as wet to the touch as the skin of the last catch.

Why are you blind to this?

Why are you blind to me and
my love of shining as brightly
as the wild flowers
you kicked to the shadows until
we grew again,
but as weeds.

Rotten Streets of Gold

I stomp the pavement.
Chicken bones cracking beneath
size ten
history writers,
soles smeared in discarded beast excrement.

Takeaway grease dancing around my nasal concha
carried by the same flickering winds
that tear brittle autumnal leaves
from branch,
earthwards
leaving them naked and lacking nourishment.
Their red hues fading,
devastating the purity
of gum and butt stained streets
with their natural shapes.

My scarf whips behind
as I stride past
the Tip Toe Wine Bar and Restaurant,
past the boys in the barbers
wanting to be men,
sat behind condensation soaked windows
having their fluffy beards shaved,
unaware
of the despair of those
in the tower blocks and bungalows

charged with fury
at having no fuel for their bellies
or radiators.
I hold on to my woollen hat
as I begin to run,
lactic acid swallowing me
as I stretch myself to
catch up with the sense of community
and friendship
that has escaped us.

We own this city,
yet we let it fall to disrepair.
We must cup our rioted,
rotten streets
in our hands
and give security,
from money lenders
and milk snatchers,
to nourish bonds re-made
and lives rebuilt.

You Dropped a Bomb to Kill All the Radical Thinkers

I was taught to question
everyone,
but you.
You held all the knowledge
and I none.
Your preaching left me ill prepared
to conquer the demons that prowled the avenues of my
future,
because when I shared what I knew,
people questioned me.
I told them you told me,
but that didn't wash.
Half ideas,
that you shared as gospel,
were all I had to dine on
and it wasn't enough to satisfy the hunger
after I'd seen what was beyond the doors you left open for
me.
If your gift to me,
when I left your hallways,
was free entry into a dirty civilisation,
then I'd rather have been left to barbarism.

Gratitude

We don't own the land,
the soil that slips between our toes
as we plough our sweat into the earth,
it is not ours to deny anyone.
It may nurture the sharp thrusts of life
from its crumbly terra firma
the leaves that fight to grasp at first light
and sprout from the darkness
to make our meals—
but we never thank it.

Instead we divide,
sticks marking the mud
tearing families and people,
creating a societal segregation
where those with the sharper sticks,
and the longest arms,
make their empires.
It's not ours to buy or sell,
but to work and cherish.

In all good conscience,
we must invest in kind words and thanks to our Mother
so that our children,
and their children,
will be able to sweat and work
and feed their families.

The Mother

You fell,
and you never got up again.

As you lay
your bloodied knuckles curled,
each beat sprayed claret a little further
until it became a trickle
and stopped.

Still.

Your pale bare hands began
to tear at the green grass
and plunge into the brown dirt.

On the surface,
often the nurturer of those
aching with displeasure and pain,
your fingers and palms now plough deeper into the earth.
Those slender pins of yours,
digging and scurrying
and taking root.

Once in
they were flat,
making a crust
strengthened in time
and weather worn.

Beneath concrete and houses,
past sewers and
your nails became stumped as they
scraped at limestone.

Fingers snaked
twisted and gurning.

Skin blistering
as you approached the core,
your arms burst wide
and you embraced the fireball within.

The fire and lava spat,
burning your flesh,
but you held on.
Squeezing so tight,
holding the light
and making it burn brighter than ever before
fuelled by your goodness. You became the mother.

Back to Town

My feet don't fit in the footsteps I carved for myself anymore.
When vice was king,
I walked with paupers.
Blind to their suffering,
the lame and hungry
making shapes under spotlights,
drinking from plastic cups
in underground clubs next to me
and not a word of comfort or friendship
or mourning for the first life we were escaping
was shared.

Now I'm back,
overdosing on bygones,
I fall to my knees
and throw up my memories
of those dances in the incandescent moonlight of youth
over the grey concrete
that made up the walls of my home.
In the death of those days we shared will walk the glory
of my children
as they sing and kick-start days with nights before
in a land that is free.
Before they live life
and life again
and make memories of their own.

Lost at Sea

The water will always carry me home,
bloated and forgotten,
past the docks
and down the Humber.

Big wheels
litter the beach side,
bulbs twinkling,
winking suggestively,
as my body evacuates itself
into the brown Roman waters.

On the boardwalk,
past ice cream stains on the pavement
and teary children,
couples and friends stroll arm in arm
shuffling to the side to avoid the dogs
scurrying around for treats,
and they only narrowly miss the
Technicolor rock sticking out
from wooden market stalls.

Faded,
sun bleached and
wind washed,
selling buckets and spades.

As I pass under the pier
I see feet,
varying in size,
and tubs full of pennies
swinging by their side.
Ready to be fed
into the ravenous slots.

Bumper cars crash
as I arrive
back into the sunlight,
beyond the Victorian icon.

Soon I'm picking up pace,
floating past
industrial chimneys
and overflow sewage pipes.
Covered in nappies and broken condoms—
the second making the first a necessity—
I stop.

Tangled in weeds,
unable,
unwilling to free myself
and face the blue unknown,
I rest in the brown
and I seep my gases and
sink.

Asleep in the silt,
I spend my days, watching boats go by.

Promenade

Some time ago now
I stood above the grey waves of the North Sea,
as it churned into a white froth
violently meeting with the silted water of the Humber
as the wooden slats of Cleethorpes pier creaked below me.
I step onto the promenade,
bleached with stepped in chips,
which has a cycle path
that goes nowhere.
Men in flat caps,
and women with dyed hair under shawls,
stroll
tentatively towards the end of the pathway.
They see more than me though,
and that's why they take their time
holding back from arriving at the end.
Because they can't turn back.
While the young rush back and forth
in a flurry of excitement at laps of the land yet to happen.
Candy floss and candy cane
thrust out of wooden slatted shelters
on sun stained plastic shelving—
Two for a pound comes the cry
as children jump at bags of sugar woven together
aimed at rotting teeth and making bellies ache.
I look out towards the sea,
but before me I see

beach balls fly
and donkey bray
on the blue flagged sands
where families sit
and the little ones play with buckets
and it distracts from the empty surf
knocking frantically and regularly on the beach
seeking attention.
And though I'm not old,
there should be more summers
and winters with the wind whipping and reddening my
cheeks,
it's time to take my stroll.
Toward the end of the prom where the light railway will take
me to the world's smallest pub
and I'll raise a toast to those still chasing
back and forth
but not seeing anything,
forgetting that one day
they'll take this stroll.

FIVE

Family Tree

I am the painter,
christening walls with emulsion
colour chosen by keen eyed owner,
of the property where I stand.
My ankles ache after a day up ladders.

I am the shop worker who
for many years,
gave her life to bringing up children
and developing the next generation.

I am a joiner,
who measures by sight,
a hairdresser who sheers locks.
I am the hospital worker
delivering food to the sick,
and I am worn,
smelting man of steel fuelled by strong pints at lunch.

I am the fisherman,
the feeder of the community.
I am the musician
taken by a bursting balloon in the chest.

I lived as you,
but grew,
like a blue wing-tipped butterfly

ripping at the security of my tightly wound chrysalis,
and despite how beautiful the making of the caterpillar may
have been,
it's better this way.
And maybe,
one day,
someone will say:
I am the poet who . . .

The Captain

I'll remember your dying day
on my dying day.

I wept,
inconsolably,
at the first I had lost.

I mourned,
eating processed fish and chips
with al dente garden peas
out of a plastic tray,
on my parents' bed.

I think it was a pound,
or maybe two,
from the local Spar shop.

The tray was cream,
and separated into individual compartments for each element
of the meal,
the peas were green,
just.

The fish,
not shaped like we know fish to be
and it may have not even been fish,
was battered
but wet from the microwave.

And the chips,
soggy too,
but comforting in the absoluteness of their insignificance in
the world.

Those chips.

There,
then gone,
but living on
in the memory of an eleven-year-old boy who'll always wish
he'd asked more questions
and held on that little bit tighter when he said the final
goodbye.

But he didn't know it was the last.

I didn't know.

For days I nestled in the bed spread
of my mum and dad
learning to understand,
and to hate,
the fact that
I'd never see you again.

All I had left was an empty try
but by chance,
I looked up,
and you looked down.

Hummingbird

Your hummingbird wings
flutter,
flustered,
firing warning shots of cold air
to fight off
a clear view of
your fearful tenderness
as you birth words
in front of my eyes,
perched on the edge of your nest.
Seeing your wings flap
and you rising slightly,
only to fall back
while getting more powerful each time,
delights me.
I listen close
for a hint
that just one
of your thousand words
was spoken for me.
I cannot help but fall
out of the tree
for you.
Sitting at the feet to our world,
looking up,
and seeing your plumage
I blush and start to ponder.

What could come of my life if only,
if only,
I could spread my wings as wide as yours.
Maybe you'd notice me.

You've Been Away

It's always been my favourite part of your holidays:
when you type *my arms* into your GPS.
When you're away I paint your days.
Dances in a hole on a beach,
fear of the turquoise sea dampening your soles, and souls.
Water colours dabbing, melancholy on paper.
Climbing in the trees, walking,
skipping, from car to café.
Oil smearing with wicked joy on cloth.

Today,
clouds form the base of the canvas of your day.
Country lanes curl horizontally and
rain splatters burn a grey hue which falls vertically,
guiding you home.

Packing the memories in a suitcase,
unpacking the dirty laundry for the chores ahead.
All a distraction.
Hectic,
bursting,
holding,
kissing,
smiling.

A night of tales.

Feet to Feet

Where you dance,
I dance,
when you laugh,
I laugh,
and when you kiss,
I'm kissed.

We twirl
and swirl,
sweet flakes of pastry
wrapping around a swirling cinnamon centre,
and we're happy.

Gorging on the indulgence
of us.

Holding dearly
to the walls we've built,
home,
our love pounds
and bounces around
our rib cages.

The heartbeats
meet
when we stand close,
prancing

to the vinyl
that plays your favourite tunes.
Then as we lay the rest our heads,
love scents drift,
intertwined within the bed
our hearts slow and soften.

We sleep,
safe in the knowledge
that our love is secure,
in our home
our hearts.

Eyes Glinting Under Street-light

and then
came the smile
diving
ripping
invigorating
pointedly
feeding my wanderlust
with walks in the woods by the water
and the heady wetness of honey
splashing onto
bended knee in an alley
behind a gym
pearls hanging from each corner
where red lip clashes
with pale cheek
to draw the eye
glisten in the starlight
as they curl into a maternal grin
after daylight moonlight weeks and months of
thudding alone
if rash pure
late to the game
for the forever joy of days together
but a light before
the darkness of the silent
infinity
bite your lip

and think of England
kiss goodbye to your days
my nights

Valentine

I can't conceive
of a dawn breaking
without your smile illuminating my day.
As we build our bond
ever stronger
through kisses and pillow talk,
our sunshine creeps
across the lands we walk
and the skies we conquer.
My valentine each day of the year,
I will hold you,
and cherish us,
and we'll flourish.

It Took Four Footsteps to Circumnavigate the World

The first,
a catastrophic breakaway
from a childhood,
full of joy and physical exertion on the playing fields
of the village where I grew,
tucked away between the sea and the steel mills,
with wild flowers staining my shins with pollen as I ran, and
forcing the bees to give chase.
I'd run and run not realising that there was only one finish
line,
and I'd not see that for years to come,
though I saw many break through the tape.

The second,
I stood bare,
alone,
outside a building in a town I'd only been to twice,
a communist style tower block became my home
where no wild flowers grew,
so I grabbed my wallet
and planted some.
Colourful friendships
matched with vibrant exploration of sex and drink and books
from the past
which we used to guide our tiptoe attitude to the present.

The third,
the struggle to establish
a life beyond the walls of education
and self-contained pleasure
where the biggest shock was having so much time to
remember,
and consider.
I slept on beds borrowed in the form of sofas, concrete,
benches,
and fought to gain foothold.
I came and went,
back to step one only to have it shattered in a heart aching
heartbeat,
and I couldn't afford to redo step two,
but at times there seemed no way forward.
Standing in an office,
daring to bark my wishes, my aspirations,
I achieved security,
and stepped back from the ledge.

Then I flew,
plumage blustering in the wind of life passing me by,
and without my knowledge I grew and threw off the shackles
of the amateurish approach that I'd taken before,
I became a man I could face in the mirror.

The forth,
you and our slow walk to cross the line together.
Each step was the happiest of times,
and to know that now,
and to have seen it then, was the greatest gift.

The Weathergirl

Stand taller,
Prouder,
and with a fiercer bark—
but keep the tenderness.
Hold on
to the smile that enchants,
the flick of the hair
and the poise of a woman
full of dexterity,
a master of life.
Ill winds once blew,
bringing aching hearts and tears,
but stay faithful to self.
You can't control the weather
and those winds
that are still blowing
the troubles
that ripped and tore
and tossed your spirit
until you thought you'd crack,
far away
and each day
becomes clearer, lighter.
Now you must grow again,
the broken limbs of life.
Create something,
built on foundations,

already years in the development
with the love
of family
and friends
to keep you strong,
unwavering.

Delight in the leaves that are blowing
in the aftermath
of that ill wind,
until the sun comes out,
because it will,
never doubt. You.

Same Page

I thought we were on the same page
but she wanted the audio book
so I bent her over
and gave her a look,
at our misery memoir.

We kissed
and I whispered
that I was in love.
We kissed
and she hissed
that she was too.

And we spent the night
back to back,
wall to wall.

In the morning
virgin light crawled our bare skin,
spindly fingers of the day
pulling at hair and goosebumps,
clawing at the bruises
of our verbal spa.

Good morning, I said.

Good morning, she said.

Back to back we got clothed
and even though she loathed,
I reached and
pulled her close
weeping into her hair
as the race to tomorrow,
that I'd lose,
began.

Into the Wind

While we were together
you began to fade
and so I
grabbed at your hips,
but you drifted into transparency,
and as I looked on, you vanished.
I considered my surrounding,
bed sheets thrown,
a layer of magnolia snow
revealing no footprints
to guide me after you.

The window rattled,
wind whispering
She went that way
and the leaves on the trees pointed me west.

I followed them,
from green up high,
to red and brown beneath my feet.

On the curb you sat,
I put my arms around your shoulders.

Was it good for you? You asked.

Note Weeper

I saw you.
Unable to control myself,
I tapped a beat
on the plaster
holding my broken self together,
and I wept your song.
Building up,
tap-tap-tap,
I reached a crescendo
and climaxed my thoughts
in a bellow
across the river,
to where you stood
naked,
exposing your tune
for my distasteful indulgence,
but no need.
I saw more
in the reflection of the seaward flow
of icy cold water,
than in the curve of your cheeks
as you smiled
and I delighted in knowing
I was the only one who'd know you
this way.
Our bodies echoed,
mine broken and hidden from view,

yours flesh bare for all to see,
and we began to dance to the heathen notes.
Ba-boom, ca-boom, da-boom.
We threw our arms
and we were merry,
uniting across the water.
Then we turned
and I hobbled away.
Looking back,
I noticed you didn't,
and our song was over.

I Cast Night on Too Many Girlfriends

My girlfriends lay the
building blocks of me.
If they were unionised,
they'd live on a picket
and strike me out of
the days of love,
and call for a truce
to end the hostilities that came
after the glory days of
mass production
died.

We are the many
they would chant.
They'd wave banners
depicting my face,
curled with a grimace
at a joke just missed,
a kiss I'd wished
had met my cheek,
and they'd take a peek
and see the charm offensive
out in force
waving batons and shields
to protect me from retribution.

We are the ninety-nine percent!

Sat alone,
in armchair padded with yesterday
and the days of speed
which passed me by,
I'd collect their grievances
of promises made,
whispered in the dark,
and learn to be a better man.

But once they're gone,
They're gone,
and even under the flag of friendship
you can't convey the truth that
they really did turn what was you,
into what could be.

So you turn,
and walk away,
never being able to say
that because of them, you are better.

You've become what they needed all along.

Half

It was that kind of night.
We kissed.
Walked together.
Said goodbye.
You got on a bus.
I walked on.
Had to.
Ended up at home.
Poured myself a half full glass of whiskey.
Sat down.
Remembered us.
Tipped it down the sink.
Poured a half empty one instead.

About the Author

Dominic Stevenson is an English-born writer with his roots in the post-industrial north of England. His aim is to take part in the global discussions surrounding societal, gender, sexual, and educational equality.

Dominic's poetry and short stories have been published in a range of print and online publications including *Litro Magazine*, *Poetry and Paint*, and *Spontaneity Arts Journal*, and his first poetry collection, *The Northern Line*, is available wherever books are sold.

Follow Dominic:
fantasticaldom.com
Twitter: @Fantastical_Dom
Facebook: facebook.com/fantasticaldom